Disruptive Transcendence

The Death of Old Business Growth Ideas & The New Strategies For Success

By: Edward A. Earle

CHAPTER ONE

The Beginning of The End

"Time changes everything except something within us which is always surprised by change."

- Thomas Hardy

One CEO to another...!one business owner to another... one entrepreneur to another.

I want to share with you content that will revolutionize the way that you view business, especially your own business... revolutionize the way that your marketplace, your competitors and your industry interacts with your business, revolutionize the way that you conduct business, and revolutionizes the way that your business makes money and the amount of money you make and the ease at which you make that money.

I want to communicate to you and the entire CEO community my message that I know how to fix the problems you are having in business, marketing, advertising, press and sales, both traditional approaches and online.

I know how to help you fix them quickly, painlessly and without emptying your bank accounts or mortgaging your future on risking propositions that you hope and pray will work out the way the business experts and newly self titled "Growth Hacker" say it is going to work out.

I know how to not only fix those problems but also fix them for good so you stop having them. So you can finally grow your business beyond them once and for all.

Problems like knowing that you are so much better at what you do than your competitors but they keep taking your business. They keep winning bids against you because they've undercut your price but are providing an inferior product or service to the

customer and there's no amount of screaming or proving to the client that you're right.

Problems like, getting your sales staff to sell at full price and stop buying into the price war and discounting your products and services while they expect full commissions on their pay checks.

Problems like figuring out (after all of these damn years) how internet and web marketing, and SEO, and social media, and video and yada, yada, yada… on and on and on… really works so you can stop paying for bullshit and start actually getting traffic and qualified leads that actually pan out into paying customers, instead of paying for consultants to push yet another program to your ever wearing growing staff, that is the "new"

program based on the "new Google parameters"… yeah, yeah, yeah.

#samestuffdifferentday.

Problems like increasing your prospect to customer conversion ration past the average of 11%… to something like 72% or more.

Problems like building legitimate brand equity in the marketplace that starts to create a tractor beam attraction to prospects, that they are compelled to come and do business with you.

This ability alone lessens the amount of marketing and advertising you need to do and gives you the opportunity to focus more on what I call Possession Oriented marketing and then onto Patriarchal Marketing formats.

This is assuming that you have correctly cultivated an understanding of what a brand is versus what you think it is and what my so-called industry "Experts" have explained it to be.

The difference is so massively far apart that if you aren't able to bet your life on it's clear description, and if you need a lifeline call in order to figure out if your logo or name, or names of your products and services are in alignment with the attributes that should make up your brand, then might I suggest that you go back and read my book, "Only The Brands Will Survive."

This way we can start on a factual foundation.

Problems like distinguishing your company from the rest of your competitors so it becomes obvious to them that you are the clear choice to do business with.

The list can go on and on and on and you know as well as I do that everything in the company is impacted by the impact of the marketing.

Everything Rises And Falls On The Marketing.

Over 20 years ago when I started in this industry of rapidly growing companies through leverage and not the "lavish lay out of loot" that traditionally accompanied the advertising and marketing agencies outline for success at the bottom of the bill; It was really easy for me to help a company separate themselves from their competition and go about monopolizing their marketplace.

My concepts of treating your advertising and marketing like a lawyer defending a client on trial worked so well it was astounding.

Not only did my concepts of building a marketing case based on specific points delineated, and then backing them up with what I called and still call marketing evidence, work for my clients. It also worked for me.

It helped me build the largest marketing agency in North America and Ranked my company on the INC 500 list three years in a row.

But the problem is...!that was a long time ago. That was during an age of what I call the "UniPlexible Marketplace."

CHAPTER TWO

The UniPlexible Marketplace

"This world is clearly emerging before our eyes. The shifts ahead, the opportunities ahead are massive."

- Carly Fiorina

A UniPlexible Marketplace" references a condition of the market that is singular. Its problems are linear in nature and the solutions are linear in nature. Think of it like simple mathematics.

$$2 + 2 = 4... \text{ every single time.}$$

You memorize the formula and you can always solve any simple equation. There really isn't any thinking or finesse required.

The marketplace has gone through so many paradigms shifts since those days that we no longer have a UniPlexible Marketplace. Believe me, I wish we did.

I made stupid amounts of money during those days as did my clients.

In a lecture I call The History Of Hype I talk about how we have gone from one paradigm shift or Sea

Change to the next to the next and on and on and on.

A paradigm shift is, according to Thomas Khun, in his influential book "The Structure of Scientific Revolutions" (1962), a change in the basic assumptions, or ruling theories that a particular community or bodies of persons share.

A paradigm shift occurs when this particular community or bodies of persons encounter anomalies that cannot be explained by the existing set of governing rules or parameters. Therefore a new set of governing rules are made.

Paradigm shifts in business or the marketplace happen when the current governing rules or parameters (what makes business grow, consumers respond, tactics to get attention or communicate to the marketplace) of a particular group (in this case, the marketplace and businesses) encounter an anomaly that cannot be explained.

Meaning simply... stuff that worked before all of a sudden doesn't work anymore and we don't know why.

From the Product Age to the Production Age to the Days of Simple Selling back before 1985, when popular sales trainers and books by Tommy Hopkins and Zig Ziglar were the rage, through those paradigm shifts into The Marketing Age where technology started to come on the scene and printers began to lose their value in the advertising game and sales people couldn't get past the answering machines.

Right at the tip of the Entrepreneurial boom and competition was rampant more than ever before; this is where I made my first fortune by solving this problem.

Then onto the Information Age when the Internet started to first explode and people began to have information digitally. Then we shifted off that paradigm as the Internet and websites became more prolific and competition increased even more significantly, people began to be "information rich and time poor."

Essentially there was so much information available on the web and it all looked and sounded exactly the same, that people stopped wanting "information".

They had all they could stand.

You know how it is...! You've been there before yourself. Search something on Google and 16 million hits come back, all which look and say the exactly same thing.

Now add in the factor that we are all pressed for time and still nothing stands out easily and quickly as the clear winner.

Enter the Emotional Economy, where I wrote the book "Only The Brands Will Survive" and several other books addressing solutions for this new Emotional Economy, and produced a few business related shows about thriving in this new business paradigm.

The crazy thing was, even at this point (back in 2005-2011) businesses were still trying to succeed in business using only the skills, philosophies and tactics from the days of simple selling. They were three paradigm shifts behind... minimum!

Those tactics were a fools notion that was no different that trying to navigate the seas with the thought that the world was flat. They might as well have been a gimmick, or the brainchild of a business development blockhead or just strategic solutions from an old time snake oil salesman.

They just didn't apply anymore and most businesses were just stagnant and not growing, and worse, dividing up the pie with more and more competitors that were coming onto the scene because of the ease of the barrier of entry due to technology.

How they ever expected to succeed with such "behind the times" battle tactics is beyond me, but for some reason CEO's in every industry still tried.

HELL… I bet you're still trying and hoping that those approaches will somehow, if done long enough and with enough ambition and enthusiasm will eventually pan out.

Well, I'm telling you… they won't.

And I think deep down inside your entrepreneurial gut, you know it.

And please understand the marketplace is so much more complicated now than it has ever been before.

Because now we have a "way" worse situation…! Enter…!the "MultiPlexible Marketplace."

CHAPTER THREE

Enter The MultiPlexible Marketplace

"Life is a moving, breathing thing. We have to be willing to constantly evolve. Perfection is constant transformation."

- Nia Peeples

If a UniPlexible Marketplace is a linear paradigm where the problems and solutions to those problems are singular in nature and straightforward and simple, then a MultiPlexible Marketplace is a paradigm or market condition where the problems are not simple and are not linear or singular.

Think about it, if businesses are still behind strategically during the age of UniPlexible Marketplace conditions and continually experience problems resulting from that lack of adaptation… then how much more perilous has this momentous shift into a MultiPlexible Marketplace become for businesses?

How much more at risk are they and how long can they hold out in a significantly more hazardous environment?

Hold out or Hole up… neither will work nor resolve until we break out and give high-priority to this demandingly urgent all- effecting shift in the way that things need to be done.

As a quick illustration of what I mean before I get into even more details of the MultiPlexible Marketplace.

Let's take a lesson from the UFC. Yes, the Ultimate Fighting Championship.

Mixed Martial Arts is the fastest growing sport in the world. By sports standards, it's also the closest thing to legal gladiatorial games as we can get minus the crowds control over life and death.

But the excitement? WOW! Electric.

Truly man –vs- man, locked in a cage and the superior man at the time comes out the victor.

There is no faking it in the Octagon.

There is nothing more real about the results of your performance than having to tap out admitting defeat or worse yet, get knocked out, knowing that you may have just become the losing end of the highlight reel.

But within the UFC, there have been many real paradigm shifts. I am speaking specifically about the types of fight strategies employed to become the UFC champion.

From the early days of boxers and strikers who gave way to the grappling arts to the shift to wrestling based ground and pound back to the strikers who rounded out their skills with jui jitsu and wrestling offense and defense. Then came the entrance of Muay Thai boxing with the clinch, knees and elbows and devastating leg kicks.

Each of these individual styles at one time or another seemed to be dominant and was considered to be the style that stood as the blueprint for reaching the top of the game.

But each style gave way to another style that exploited the current winning styles weaknesses.

Over the years a few fighters have emerged as "Complete Fighters." Fighters that were equally skilled in every discipline.

Fighters like GSP (George Saint Pierre) and Jonny Bones Jones, the current light heavyweight champ.

Jones is considered to be, what is known as a SUPER FIGHTER.

He is the very definition of the ultimate fighter. All the strengths of all of the disciplines yet none of the weaknesses.

This is now the style of success. To be a SUPER FIGHTER. This is what it takes to win and succeed in the UFC today.

And we are seeing SUPER FIGHTERS across all weight classes. Kids now grow up taking MMA lessons that include all styles, and the concept of just taking a singular style with designs on making in this sport are gone. Today kids train to be super fighters.

The metaphor is all of the singular styles are UniPlexible...!they are singular disciplines yet not dynamic. The SUPER FIGHTER is Multi-Plexible.

It is not simple. It is dynamic, every changing, 360 degrees, flowing, moving, adjusting, and evolving.

It would be insane and a sure bet for a serious beat down to think that you could go into the UFC, fighting Jonny Bones Jones the SUPER FIGHTER, with a UniPlexible fighting style like the wrestling based ground and pound of the sports early years.

The same is true for you or any business.

You need to be at minimum an Entrepreneurial Super Fighter.

A business super fighter if you will.

A management super fighter, a production super fighter, a executive super fighter, an accounting super fighter, a marketing and advertising super fighter...!a sales super fighter.

That is the reality of the shift from UniPlexible Marketplace Conditions to MultiPlexible Marketplace conditions.

You see, the facts are, something radically different has happened. Something bigger than a sea change, something that has changed the landscape.

Think of the concept of the great flood in the Bibles book of Genesis.

The waters came from the skies above and the earth opened up and released its waters.

Everything changed, the entire face of the earth change. Just like today's marketplace.

Everything has changed.

I've watched this happen. I foresaw it... and lectured about it for years.

I built strategies for businesses to protect themselves from it and succeed irrespective of it.

But they were already so many paradigm shifts behind that they couldn't keep afloat. Now they are drowning in the waters.

The Paradigm I'm talking about within this MultiPlexible Marketplace is what I call "Fractured Divergence."

This is where we find ourselves right now at this moment.

CHAPTER FOUR

Fractured Divergence… Today's Paradigm

"The complexity of things – the things within things – just seems to be endless. I mean nothing is easy, nothing is that easy and simple."

— Alice Munro

Fractured Divergence means exactly what it's component words mean combined:

Fractured: *Meaning to break and split apart.*

Divergence: *Outflowing from one origin point with no finite limits.*

Fractured Divergence is like broken glass fracturing and shattering in a million pieces, big and small, with slivers scattering everywhere and anywhere.

Some pieces you can see and some pieces you can't but you will feel the reality of their effect when you step on them.

It is a marketplace paradigm that is fracturing and spreading with no finite limitations. It will not end,

you cannot control it and it seemingly does what it wants to do with no apparent reason or justification.

The resulting problems to businesses are the same as all of the other paradigm shifts but even worse and significantly more difficult to overcome.

Fractured Divergence is Paradigm shifts within paradigm shifts.

There are way too many things to manage and guard against – it's 360 degrees, different speeds, different flows, different individuals, attacking competitors here, and then gone.

The rules of SEO are ever changing on a whim of the companies that built the structure.

Think of it as fluidity – constantly changing, new websites, new parameters, etc. Trends shifting quickly and constantly.

Once you think you may have a slight handle or grip on something to pull you safety, it gives way.

Google throws you a life-line and then six months later pulls it back in or worse, throws the entire line in the water.

You think you're saved when your rope of redemption isn't attached to anything except for the water that's pulling you under.

Then there's the matter of market Transparency.

The fact that because of the immediacy and viral nature of the web, anything that we do online is easily seen through, detected and recognized for it's

authenticity, accuracy and verity or on the opposite side, it's distortion, fabrication and fraudulence.

And this, as I stated is instantaneous due to the nature of the peoples Immediacy and connectivity. Everything and everyone is connected to everything else and everyone else.

And part of what makes that connectivity so supersonic is the accessibility of mobility.

Our mobile devices with wireless internet, can push a hilariously entertaining video to millions of viewers in hours, leaving the whole world in huge har-d- har's. It can locate a criminal fled from the scene of a crime just 20 minutes earlier by a Facebook notification complete with picture and personal dossier of criminal history.

It can validate the performance of a product through reviews and tagging others to chime in with their two-cents worth, or like so much Internet "news"... Blue Streak a line of Bullshit so fast that the boys in blue cannot respond fast enough to protect against the unjustified threats of bodily harm.

Fractured Divergence, the paradigm we now find ourselves in, is dangerous and cruel when you get it wrong. Cruel especially when you end up on the receiving end of an attack motivated by what many call Keyboard Commando Courage.

You've seen it, you've experienced it, you might have even participated in it. So I know that you understand the significance of this paradigm Fractured Divergence.

It's like fighting a Hydra. The monster of olden Greek Mythology. Cut off one head and two heads grow in its place.

Fractured Divergence is like fighting an army of Hydras.

This is why things don't work. And if you figure one part of one thing out, i.e cut off one head… two more grow in its place.

It is a game you cannot win.

It's because you are taking a UniPlexible Marketplace Approach to a MultiPlexible Marketplace Problem.

You cannot win because you will always be reacting to the marketplace, you will always be reacting to the system.

The new parameters that Google programs, and then they shift of rules when companies buy other companies, the whims and trends of a wildly emotional consumer base… on and on and on.

You are following. You are not leading.

You cannot win in that lower position.

You need to gain higher ground.

You need to Disrupt the system, Disrupt the structure, and then… Transcend it.

To be above and beyond the system or structure.

I know it sounds a little Matrix and Neo-like huh? LOL

But it is true. For as long as you are reacting to the structure and not directly connected to the marketplace then you will never be able to be in control of your success ultimately.

Because you will always be effected by the next sea change or paradigm shift.

Which in this Fractured Divergent marketplace, happens constantly. There's no way to keep up or juggle that many balls.

You are always behind and falling further behind every day. You need to have a philosophical business model that is beyond that.

Stop playing the game that you cannot win.

I will say this though; it's a brilliant maneuver and a savvy scam, because it keeps businesses like you paying money to companies like Google and so on.

It keeps money coming into agencies for video, SEO, and every other service that "today's digital marketing agencies" can charge you for, etc.

Think about it. Let's talk a little conspiracy theory here. Remember the day when as a business you were totally at the mercy of advertising media and agencies?

Without them, you could not succeed.

It kept coin in their pockets. And as things became more successful and media got better and better the costs kept going up.

Less ad time... more fees. They controlled businesses success.

Then came the Internet. A promise to break away from those media mafia types.

A promise to be able to grow free, without high fees and out from under their dominance and abusive control.

And we did for a while. But somehow, some way those "For Free" (how they promoted the internet and their positions in the very beginning) companies had to make money... they had to turn a profit.

Enter the end of the free web success.

Now once again, a few big companies own and control all of the platforms that govern our success in business based on media... the rules keep changing and once again the new media (web based not print, radio or television) is in control and we are once again at the mercy of the Advertising Media giants.

Just like before, there's no way we can win. They won't allow it.

For us to win is for them to lose.

And they are not going to let that happen.

They lost a few battles for a few years, knowing the entire time that the day would come (after we were all dependent on their structures for success, they would flip the script) and ultimately win the war.

Hence the need to understand what I am saying to you.

You need to Disrupt the structure and Transcend the structure

Then you will always be in control. You will be beyond their touch.

No matter how much technology grows and changes, it will be simple for you to grow your business to the next level.

You will be able to have a handle on your business and grow your business "AT WILL."

Which is what we are all seeking for. It's what we truly want. It is one of the main points behind why we are entrepreneurs… to control our own destiny.

CHAPTER FIVE

The Need To Disrupt & Transcend

"Fools ignore complexity. Pragmatists suffer it. Some can avoid it. Geniuses remove it."

- Alan Perlis

Let's talk about how to Disrupt & Transcend:

The concept of Disruptive Transcendence is to separate yourself and depart from current industry norms (business models) and the media structures themselves thereby growing past them, growing past their control on your success and growing beyond even your very industry itself.

To transcend the industry and it's players and become More than just a (fill in whatever your business is to the marketplace, plumber, accountant, mechanic, doctor, ect) becoming more to the marketplace and the individuals.

This concept of transcendence leaves a wake of destruction and disrupts the very industry you're in and it's participants never to be the same.

This concept makes you the shift in the paradigms or the sea changes in the industry.

Your entire philosophy about business, the marketplace and your business model even has to adapt. You need to become a business built on a MultiPlexible framework.

This adjustment is Disruptive and Transcendent.

It's not a hard adjustment. You don't have to buy all new equipment or build new buildings so-to-speak.

It's a philosophical shift.

Making the shift will disrupt the structure and go beyond it and you will not be at the mercy of the media.

You will disrupt or destroy the old model of business – the way it's done and has been done for what seems like forever.

Product and service combinations, customer connectivity (most importantly) all enhanced significantly.

You will leave a wake so big and tough to handle that others will find it difficult to operate anymore.

Similar to how the light bulb essentially killed off the in home kerosene market. One day Rockefeller is making a killing on Kerosene and the next... nothing.

The opportunity for that kind of market dominance is real, just like in the old days of industry without of course; the greed, corruption and corporate conspiracies that actually allow the titans to amass their masses of treasure and assets.

This kind of ascendency is first a conquering strategy and then a governing strategy.

This is based on Leadership.

Based on what I call Patriarchal Marketing and the building of the HOUSE and by developing FOLLOWERS, the later two being acronyms for business concepts that create Disruptive Transcendence, which well get into a little detail in just a minute.

In order to make this transition you need to also comprehend that most all business and most

certainly yours, is based on the business model of Promise 4 Profits.

This is a very linear and UniPlexible Marketplace business concept. It's not dynamic. Simply put, you:

- Find a need and fill it

- Make a list of your customers needs and desires

- See how you can fill them

And then when you go to market, you communicate a promise to the marketplace that says it's better that they buy from you versus any of their competitors.

If they end up purchasing or doing business with

you, what they pay minus the cost to fulfill the product or service is your Profit.

You have Made a Promise to the Marketplace and if they purchase... YOU PROFIT.

Think about this for just a minute.

YOU PROFIT.

The marketplace does not profit. Not in anyway at all. The reason why is that, they received exactly (let's hope so anyway) what they were promised if they were to pay you and conduct business with you.

Nothing really more than that. There is no equity built into that relationship at all.

Compare that to your other competitors. You and they are essentially exactly the same.

If that is the case, how then can you possibly stand out in this MultiPlexible Marketplace under this Fractured Divergence paradigm?

In order to Transcend you have to go far beyond the accepted linear business model of Promise 4 Profit.

By assuming the Patriarchal role I've started to introduce, you transcend the traditional customer/business relationship and take on a philosophical Adoptive Child Approach.

This starts the process of creating a disruption in your industry.

By simply adjusting your view of the relationship you have with the marketplace, which will adjust your growth strategies and tactics, which will adjust the response of the marketplace to your business and ultimately adjust your growth and profit significantly.

More sales, more profit, faster, less expense, protected from competitive attacks, not controlled by the media structure, etc.

There's a psychology that is the legitimate undercurrent of what drives the marketplace that you need to not only be aware of, but fully grasp if you are to positively employ my supposition of Disruptive Transcendence.

And that psychology is this...

"What we think or believe we lack determines the person that we become."

It is human instinct to be compelled to desire things that we cannot have by ourselves or given our current set of circumstances.

This foundational human trait drives this natural core response.

Which is...

There is a struggle in the human psyche to maintain the balance between these two innate human objectives:

1. Power and Personal Aggrandizement

2. Social Feeling, Acceptance, Recognition and Togetherness

Let me state that again and please listen intently so that it sinks so deep inside your thought processes that it changes the core of what drives your every thought when it comes to business development.

There is a struggle in the human psyche to maintain the balance between these two innate human objectives:

1. Power and Personal Aggrandizement

2. Social Feeling, Acceptance, Recognition and Togetherness

These two things go far beyond your linear business offerings and are the very core of what truly motivates people's actions.

In order to transcend, you have to have a business model that allows you to provide both of these objectives to your marketplace. And in doing so it needs to be obvious to them that they can achieve or have the hope achieving these two objectives with you.

Doing this will carry you to the top of the minds list of what's important, or T.O.M.

Understand, the mind only has so many (very few) top slots in its memory T.O.M (Top of Mind)

Even if you become the very best in your industry (fill in your business type) you will only arrive at the top of a list within your given category of business. And that category of business itself, is most likely not at the top of the minds over all.

Those slots are reserved for things that are the most emotionally based (good or bad) scenarios given an individuals life.

These are things that have to rank the HIGHEST on my levels of the S.T.R.E.S.S chart and B.S. Scale.

I'll save the details on those acronyms for the actual hardback version of this book.

As an example is, I have a good friend that owns an HVAC company and through using good marketing strategies he has become one of the most successful companies of his kind in his area.

His customers love him, his margins are strong, his competition cowers when it comes time to bid against him... but given all of that, he is nowhere near the Top Of Mind list, although he is at the top of the list for HVAC companies.

You might think... *"I'm ok with that. He's successful"*.

Yes but the market has shifted and will always be shifting. He is vulnerable and still at the mercy of the media structures. His collateral can be copied and he can be taken down.

He is a very successful UniPlexible Business. A very successful Promise 4 Profit business.

But in a MultiPlexible Marketplace, a Fractured Divergence paradigm, he is open to attack. And because the marketplace is whimsical and their attention spans are like gnats, he is never assured that his position is secure.

Not to say that you ever want to rest on your laurels, but he feels like he is always conquering the same ground every day.

As it will always be using Promise 4 Profit, UniPlexible Marketplace approaches.

Now the word has spread and his competition has wised up and is following his lead. He is losing business to good competitors who now have copied his way of communicating to the marketplace.

The Cycle of Communication concept from my book "Only The Brands Will Survive" is a good lesson in this type of situation.

You can grab that book on Amazon also.

If he doesn't adapt… if he doesn't Disrupt and Transcend, he will be run over by more and more aggressive competitors. And he will spend himself into the ground trying to maintain a losing battle.

Are you beginning to understand that you can never achieve that level of Top Of Mind importance by filling linear traditionally or business specific needs and wants? Promise 4 Profit. It is a UniPlexible Marketplace business model in a MultiPlexible Marketplace.

All UniPlexible Marketplace Advertising is "Promise" Oriented

And now that we have shifted into a MultiPlexible Marketplace you also need to really recognize that.

The marketplace doesn't trust advertising and marketing promises.

No matter how loud you shout it to the marketplace (Bigger and bigger advertising promises, risk free, bonuses with purchase, free offers, lower prices, etc) and no matter how much you shout it out to the marketplace. (frequency and numbers of media channels, SEO, Website, Social Media, YouTube, etc)

The Cycle of Profit

You must provide Profit to the marketplace but first you must build equity before you can make a withdraw. Before you can expect them to read, listen or view your content... expect a response to your marketing... spend time with you on the phone... come into the store... be willing to be honest about their problems... trust your solutions… eliminate the other competitors and give you the transaction… tell their friends… you have to use their influence to bring others into YOUR HOUSE.

You cannot expect any other connectivity if you do not first build equity by reversing the flow of profit and initiate the flow of profit first to the marketplace before you receive profit.

The building of that equity is part of Patriarchal Marketing.

CHAPTER SIX

Shifting To Patriarchal Marketing

"A leader is one who knows the way, goes the way and shows the way."

- John C. Maxwell

Let's talk about the Definition of a Patriarch:

A Patriarch is someone who exercises paternal care over other persons, a paternal protector and provider.

Think to yourself about someone in your life who has filled or fills that role in your life.

Describe that person. Make a list in your mind, combined with the memories of the attributes and actions of Patriarchal person.

When it comes to shifting your business model to align with today's marketplace paradigm, you are the Patriarch over the Marketplace.

You, as a leader should exercise paternal care over the marketplace. The entire marketplace is your family... your children. Your job is to:

- Protect them

- Provide for them

- Preside over them

How do you accomplish this in a business sense?

In helping you resolve this in a business related strategy and tactics of marketing message and sales deployment you will begin to fill those two psychological objectives that every single healthy person on this planet craves instinctively.

You now have the ability to become Top Of Mind… not just the top of the categorical list of your industry… but actually Top Of Mind.

Doing this allows transcendence beyond your typical relational role with the marketplace and this in turn disrupts the paradigm of business development models in your industry.

Executing this is not just philosophical… it is a customized plan developed by my private agency Bulb Breakers, specifically for your company that entails strategy and tactics across all appropriate media channels.

The strategies we implement are powerful but are all contained within the actual tactics being deployed.

Strategies like:

- Genesis Growth

- 4i SWOT

- Our 4-D Approach

- Discover –!Discredit –!Distribute - Defection

- 5-C's of a Marketplace Takeover

- Company – Competitors – Competitors – Connectors – Consumers - Crowd

- The Circles of Innovation

- T.E.M.P.T

- F.O.L.L.O.W.E.R

- The H.O.U.S.E

Just to name a few.

Let me just validate the concepts we've been talking about with an important study and finding from the IBM Institute for Business Value.

It's called *"What Do Chief Executives Really Want? What one Leadership competency do they value over any and all others?"*

Even though this study was directed at employee and executive ranks within a company, it's the reasons "Why?" they value this one attribute that validate my concept of Disruptive Transcendence.

So, what do chief executive officers really want?

Beginning of IBM Article -

The answer bears important consequences for management as well as companies' customers and shareholders. The qualities that a CEO values most in the company team set a standard that affects everything from product development and sales to the long-term success of an enterprise.

There is compelling new evidence that CEOs' priorities in this area are changing in important ways. According to a new survey of 1,500 chief executives conducted by IBM's Institute for Business Value, CEOs identify "creativity" as the most important leadership competency for the successful enterprise of the future.

That's creativity—not operational effectiveness, influence, or even dedication. Coming out of the worst economic downturn in their professional lifetimes, when managerial discipline and rigor ruled the day, this indicates a remarkable shift in attitude. It is consistent with the study's other major finding: Global complexity is the foremost issue confronting these CEOs and their enterprises.

The chief executives see a large gap between the level of complexity coming at them and their confidence that their enterprises are equipped to deal with it.

Until now creativity has generally been viewed as fuel for the engines of research or product development, not the essential leadership asset that must permeate an enterprise.

What's Needed? Creative Disruption

Much has happened in the past two years to shake the historical assumptions held by the women and men who are in charge.

In addition to global recession, the century's first decade heightened awareness of the issues surrounding global climate change and the interplay between natural events and our supply chains for materials, food, and even talent.

In short, CEOs have experienced the realities of global integration. The world is massively interconnected—economically, socially, and politically—and operating as a system of systems.

So what does this look like at the level of customer relationships? For too many enterprises, the answer is that their customers are increasingly connected, but not to them.

Against that backdrop of interconnection, interdependency, and complexity, business leaders around the world are declaring that success requires fresh thinking and continuous innovation at all levels of the organization.

As they step back and reassess, CEOs have seized upon creativity as the necessary element for enterprises that must reinvent their customer relationships and achieve greater operational dexterity.

In face-to-face interviews with our consultants, they said creative leaders do the following:

- **Disrupt the status quo.** Every company has legacy products that are both cash–and sacred–cows. Often, the need to perpetuate the success of these products restricts innovation within the enterprise, creating a window for competitors to advance competing innovations. As CEOs tell us that fully one-fifth of revenues will have to come from new sources, they are recognizing the requirement to break with existing assumptions, methods, and best practices.

- **Disrupt existing business models.** CEOs who select creativity as a leading competency are far more likely to pursue innovation through business model change. In keeping with their view of accelerating complexity, they are breaking with traditional strategy-planning cycles in favor of continuous, rapid-fire shifts and adjustments to their business models.

- **Disrupt organizational paralysis.** Creative leaders fight the institutional urge to wait for completeness, clarity, and stability before making decisions. To do this takes a combination of deeply held values, vision, and conviction–combined with the application of such tools as analytics to the historic explosion of information. These drive decision making that is faster, more precise, and even more predictable.

Taken together, these recommendations describe a shift toward corporate cultures that are far more transparent and entrepreneurial.

They are cultures imbued with the belief that complexity poses an opportunity, rather than a threat.

They hold that risk is to be managed, not avoided, and that leaders will be rewarded for their ability to build creative enterprises with fluid business models, not absolute ones.

Something significant is afoot in the corporate world.

In response to powerful external pressures and the opportunities that accompany them, CEOs are signaling a new direction.

They are telling us that a world of increasing complexity will give rise to a new generation of

leaders that make creativity the path forward for successful enterprises.

End of IBM Article --

Chapter Seven

The Dawning Of a New Day

"A pessimist sees the difficulty in every opportunity; and optimist sees the opportunity is every difficulty."

- Winston Churchill

The facts are simple. CEO's of major corporations recognize today's MultiPlexible Marketplace... They recognize today's Fractured Divergence Paradigm.

They recognize that Creativity, especially disruptive creativity is what is needed to for them to personally connect in an already connected world.

The problem remains.

How do they find people like that?

How to do find employees like that?

Are there any out there?

Or, are those people taken the road less traveled, the road of entrepreneurialism?

And if major corporations with all the money and perks to pitch, present and pass on to these creatively disruptive types, find it laborious to scratch a few out of the labor pool... then how in the hell are you, the small to mid-sized business owner going to come up with one.

These types are the most valuable assets big corporations and CEO's can stumble upon.

I can assure that they are not going to just hand them over to you, nor do you have the "extra gravy" that would allow you to haggle or dicker for their trust and commitment.

But, the fact remains you need them. Or, do you actually really need them?

Do you need them or do you just need the disruptive creativity?

It's the later. You need the talent not the talented.

That's where we come in.

Your job is not to be the expert, that's our job.

Your job is to do what you do best. Spend your time doing what you do best, which is to provide the best product and or service.

We will build the collateral case to validate that you are the one to do business with. We will execute the program and together will can Disrupt the structure and Transcend the industry.

The result will be an immediate stop to:

- Failing to grow the way and at the rate you want to?

- Stop getting killed in the marketplace?

- Stop the marketing from not working?

- Stop your salespeople from failing to get in the door?

- Stop being subject to the fluctuations of the marketplace and the whims of the consumers?

And... add whatever other struggles you are having with growing your business to the list.

CONCLUSION...

I don't need statistics to prove to you that we've been in the worst economy that any of us have ever experienced since becoming an entrepreneur, business owner or executive.

And there's a lot of reasons, both legitimate and finger pointing at who and what's to blame.

Regardless of any report in the media (print, television or online) this one simple fact remains.

The last almost decade has been a purging of the over proliferation of businesses that was past their prime, were poorly planned upstarts, or whose value propositions couldn't hold out against more persistent entrepreneurs who could pull themselves up and hold on to their pursuit of profits.

Those who have lasted have refined their passion, dug deep into their will, and strengthened their spirit of success. Those are they who have outlasted the outing.

And for those of us who are still here, let me say;

"The economic purging of the last decade has created one of the greatest opportunities in the history of capitalism."

I liken this purging to the bible story of Noah and The Great Flood.

The waters have receded. Only the strong have survived (or have been bailed out by the taxpayers of this great nation.

They don't count. LOL). And as we all walk off our arks, it is our opportunity to start again.

The world is ours.

The marketplace can be taken at will. There are no more lines or boundaries. The marketplace is up for grabs.

The marketplace is as open as the old west. All the land is up for grabs.

Consumers are ready and willing for new relationships with companies who understand

branding, marketing, advertising, press, sales and so forth in this new paradigm.

That's what Disruptive Transcendence is all about.

Let me teach you and provide you the strategies, tactics and support to help you take advantage of this great opening.

Let me teach you how to Disrupt and Transcend.

The results will be Monopolizing Your Marketplace with ease. Here's just a few of the specifics:

- You'll be able to capture mass amounts of leads. Not only single individuals but groups as well.

- Quickly nurture those leads into enormous customer transactions.

- Discredit those competitors that don't play fair.

- Getting total connectivity with the marketplace by creating community based interaction.

- Creating a universal feeling that your business is the one to go to.

- Even getting non-prospects on your side and referring your business.

In short, understanding and implementing my Disruptive Transcendence strategies will grow your business fast, as big as you want, when you want, at will, without increased expense or liability.

It is the magic bullet we as entrepreneurs are looking for.

You just need to be willing to walk away from some old concepts of business development that haven't been valid for over 30 years and even a few that are new as of the last 5 years, but have gone out just as fast as they came in.

You need to reside yourself to the fact that the majority of all these so called experts on subjects like SEO, Online Press, Social Media, Web Strategy, etc… are not experts and definitely not people who have created personal financial success using the strategies that they promote and have somehow become very popular for.

These individuals (I call them "paper guru's" and now "digital guru's") are responsible for sucking in CEO's, marketing managers and sales managers the world over at every level of business and diversity of enterprise.

This proliferation of fake, half-baked truth strategies about business growth – purported by these false profit prophets has the world standing and kneeling at their feet in devotion.

They are not only sacrificing their hard earned money to these paper guru's and their fanciful, fairy tale plans, programs and procedures – but, they are ultimately sacrificing their companies success and their personal lifestyle.

This vomiting of venom against those in my industry is an attempt to shake you and wake you as to the reality of these promotional promises of mass proceeds.

It's not that those types of tactical approaches don't work or that they can't work.

I'm just saying that the people who have set themselves up as "experts" are NOT the ones that know how to make them work.

And that you need to stop being enticed and googly-eyed over the allure of shining objects reflecting off the sun of slackers success.

In the coming chapters I will outline legitimately how to take over your marketplace.

This is what I do for companies in every type of industry and at every economic level. This content is real.

And it really works.

For those CEO's who want to secure their future with solid strategy and stop wasting time, money and opportunity.

Remember… each time you blow it in the marketplace with bad marketing, advertising, sales and PR… you fall further and further behind.

You leave a bad impression and lose more and more credibility.

It's a downward spiral that can only be corrected by correct strategy.

It's that damn simple.

No different than any other decision or any other relationship.

If you keep making mistakes with people, there will shortly come a time where you have bankrupted your trust bank, as Stephen Covey would say.

And it doesn't matter how many times you metaphorically apologize to the marketplace.

It starts to fall on deaf ears and then they turn the proverbial blind eye.

And this is not only an impact that affects the marketplace, but it affects your employees, both salaried and commissioned alike.

It affects your leadership ability and their belief in you as the captain of the ship. They have attached their hopes and dreams to the set of your sail.

If you keep floundering around amidst the sea each and every time you reset the compass to the destined destiny to which they were promised when they "put in"… there will soon be mutiny.

And you won't notice it at first.

They won't come right out and attack you, bind you and make you walk the plank.

Oh, no sir.

It will sneak up on you.

They will start by not putting in their full effort each day on the job. They will become lax in their duties.

Customer service will suffer, sales will suffer, compromises on full price will be made.

And in the end...!after months and months and possibly even years of flailing as a business, then they will completely abandon you on some island as they sail away with your assets to your competition.

They will take their talent and your intellectual property and your clients and board another ship in whose captain they have renewed trust.

And you know that every word I am saying is true.

So let's agree to stop pretending right now and go forward and get our compass and strategy right on, right from the get go.

Fair enough?

Contact us and let's get started.

Thanks for reading,

EDward

www.ingramcontent.com/pod-product-compliance
Lightning Source LLC
Chambersburg PA
CBHW070456220526
45466CB00004B/1849